recite Quran

straightaway

Fauzan Baharudin

First published in the UK Jan 2015

In depth meaning and translation can be obtained from
Saheeh International flash book http://www.quranabc.com/
quran. Exact pronunciation of each verse can also be
studied online via quran.com. Please note that the author
have no association with these two sources in any way.

email: fazsimplify@gmail.com

Special Thanks

My beloved wife Myra and son Hud for
their support and patience throughout
completion of this first book - many more
to come inshaAllah.

faz

read this first

This book is not a substitute to the holy Quran. Instead, it is an excellent starting point for Quran recitation.

This book will hugely benefit parents and teachers introducing Quran and _s_alat to young children, reverts to Islam and generally non-Arabic readers.

The transliteration of each verse have been matched very closely to the real pronunciation however readers are <u>strongly</u> advised to learn about tajweed and listen to audio from alternative sources in parallel to using this book.

Please note that the arabic letters and phonetic guide are placed at the end of this book for easy reference.

contents

Chapter 1: Surat Al-Fātiħah (The Opener) - 7 aayats in total

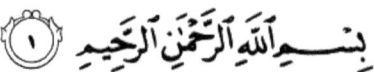

bism*illaah*ir rohmaanir rohiim

In the name of Allah, the Entirely Merciful, the Especially Merciful

al hamdu l*illaah*i robbil 'aalamiin

[All] praise is [due] to Allah, Lord of the worlds

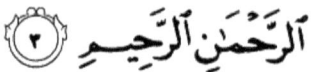

ar rohmaanir rohiim

The Entirely Merciful, the Especially Merciful

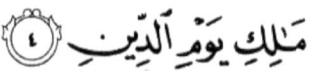

maaliki yaumid diin

Sovereign of the Day of Recompense

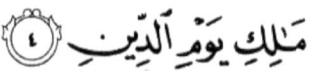

iyyaaka na'budu wa iyyaaka nasta'iin

It is You we worship and You we ask for help

4

Chapter 1: Surat Al-Fātiĥah (The Opener) - 7 aayats in total

ihdinas sirootol mustaqiim

Guide us to the straight path

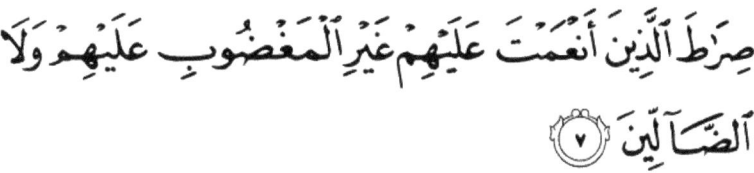

sirootol ladziina an'amta 'alaihim ghoiril maghduubi 'alaihim walad doooliiin

The path of those upon whom You have bestowed favor, not of those who have evoked [Your] anger or of those who are astray

Allah does not charge a soul except [with that within] its capacity. It will have [the consequence of] what [good] it has gained, and it will bear [the consequence of] what [evil] it has earned. "Our Lord, do not impose blame upon us if we have forgotten or erred. Our Lord, and lay not upon us a burden like that which You laid upon those before us. Our Lord, and burden us not with that which we have no ability to bear. And pardon us; and forgive us; and have mercy upon us. You are our protector, so give us victory over the disbelieving people" (2:286 Al-Baqarah)

Chapter 93: Surat Ađ-Đuħaá (The Morning Hours) - 11 aayats in total

بسم الله الرحمن الرحيم

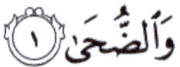

wa<u>d</u> <u>d</u>uhaa

By the morning brightness

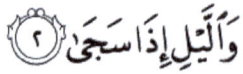

wal laili idzaa sajaa

And [by] the night when it covers with darkness

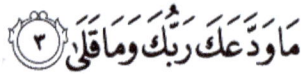

maa wad da'aka robbuka wa maa qolaa

Your Lord has not taken leave of you, [O Muhammad], nor has He detested [you]

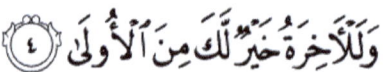

wa lal aakhirotu khoirul laka minal uulaa

And the Hereafter is better for you than the first [life]

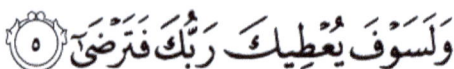

wa lasaufa yu'<u>t</u>iika robbuka fatar<u>doo</u>

And your Lord is going to give you, and you will be satisfied

Chapter 93: Surat Aḍ-Ḍuḥaá (The Morning Hours) - 11 aayats in total

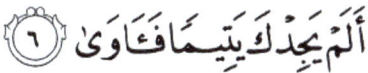

alam yajidka yatiiman~fa aawaa

Did He not find you an orphan and give [you] refuge

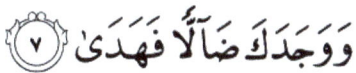

wa wajadaka dooollan~fa hadaa

And He found you lost and guided [you]

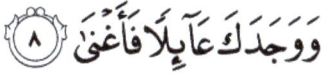

wa wajadaka 'aaa ilan~fa aghnaa

And He found you poor and made [you] self-sufficient

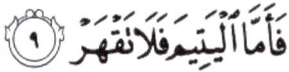

fa ammal yatiima falaa taq har

So as for the orphan, do not oppress [him]

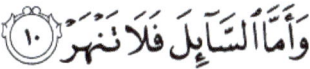

wa ammas saaa ila falaa tan har

And as for the petitioner, do not repel [him]

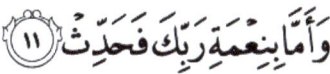

wa ammaa bini'mati robbika fahaddith

But as for the favor of your Lord, report [it]

Chapter 94: Surat Ash-Sharh (The Relief) - 8 aayats in total

بسم الله الرحمن الرحيم

أَلَمْ نَشْرَحْ لَكَ صَدْرَكَ ﴿١﴾

alam nashroh laka sodrok

Did We not expand for you, [O Muhammad], your breast

وَوَضَعْنَا عَنكَ وِزْرَكَ ﴿٢﴾

wa wado'naa 'an~ka wizrok

And We removed from you your burden

ٱلَّذِىٓ أَنقَضَ ظَهْرَكَ ﴿٣﴾

al ladziii an~qodo zohrok

Which had weighed upon your back

وَرَفَعْنَا لَكَ ذِكْرَكَ ﴿٤﴾

wa rofa'naa laka dzikrok

And raised high for you your repute

فَإِنَّ مَعَ ٱلْعُسْرِ يُسْرًا ﴿٥﴾

fa inna ma'al 'usri yusroo

For indeed, with hardship [will be] ease

Chapter 94: Surat Ash-Sharh (The Relief) - 8 aayats in total

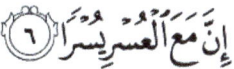

inna ma'al 'usri yusroo

Indeed, with hardship [will be] ease

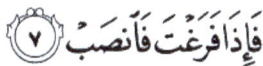

fa idzaa faroghta fan~sob

So when you have finished [your duties], then stand up [for worship]

wa ilaa robbika farghob

And to your Lord direct [your] longing.

And [it is] a Qur'an which We have separated [by intervals] that you might recite it to the people over a prolonged period. And We have sent it down progressively
(17:106 Al-Isra`)

Chapter 95: Surat At-Tīn (The Fig) - 8 aayats in total

بسم الله الرحمن الرحيم

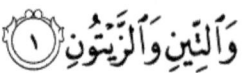

wat tiini waz zaituun

By the fig and the olive

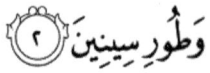

wa *t*uuri siiniin

And [by] Mount Sinai

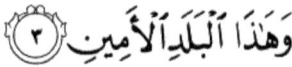

wa *h*aadzal baladil amiin

And [by] this secure city [Makkah]

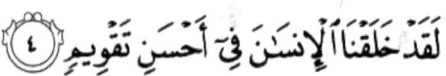

laqod kholaqnal in~saana fiii ahsani taqwiim

We have certainly created man in the best of stature

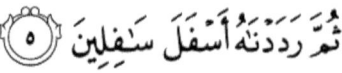

thumma rodadnaa*h*u asfala saafiliin

Then We return him to the lowest of the low

Chapter 95: Surat At-Tīn (The Fig) - 8 aayats in total

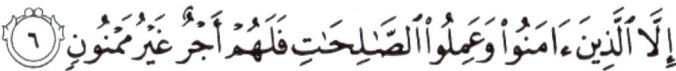

illal ladziina aamanuu wa'amilus _s_oolihaati fala_h_um ajrun ghoiru mamnuun

Except for those who believe and do righteous deeds, for they will have a reward uninterrupted

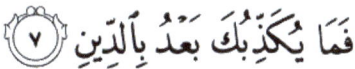

fa maa yukadzzibuka ba'du biddiin

So what yet causes you to deny the Recompense

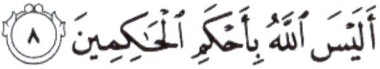

alais_allaah_u bi ahkamil haakimiin

Is not Allah the most just of judges?

Allah has created every [living] creature from water. And of them are those that move on their bellies, and of them are those that walk on two legs, and of them are those that walk on four. Allah creates what He wills. Indeed, Allah is over all things competent (24:45 An-Nur)

Chapter 96: Surat Al-`Alaq (The Clot)- 19 aayats in total

بسم الله الرحمن الرحيم

iqro*k* bismi robbikal ladzii kholaq
Recite in the name of your Lord who created

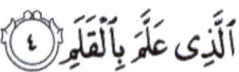

kholaqol in~saana min 'alaq
Created man from a clinging substance

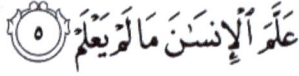

iqro*k* wa robbukal akrom
Recite, and your Lord is the most Generous

al ladzii 'allama bil qolam
Who taught by the pen

'allamal in~saana maa lam ya'lam
Taught man that which he knew not

Chapter 96: Surat Al-`Alaq (The Clot)- 19 aayats in total

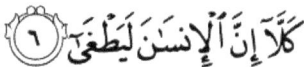

kallaaa innal in~saana laya*t*ghoo

No! [But] indeed, man transgresses

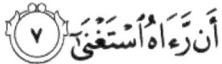

ar ro aa*h*us taghnaa

Because he sees himself self-sufficient

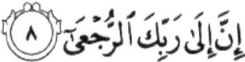

inna ilaa robbikar ruj'aa

Indeed, to your Lord is the return

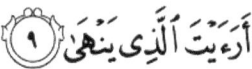

aro aital ladzii yan *h*aa

Have you seen the one who forbids

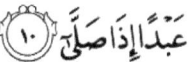

'abdan idzaa *s*ollaa

A servant when he prays

aro aita in~kaana 'alal *h*udaa

Have you seen if he is upon guidance

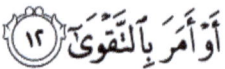

aw amara bit taqwaa

Or enjoins righteousness

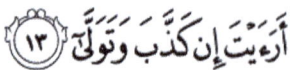

aro aita in~kadzzaba wa tawallaa

Have you seen if he denies and turns away

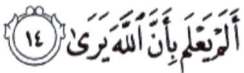

alam ya'lam bi ann*allaah*a yaroo

Does he not know that Allah sees

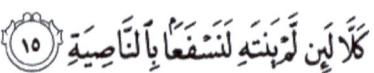

kallaa la illam yan~ta*h*i lanasfa'am bin naa*s*ia*h*

No! If he does not desist, We will surely drag him by the forelock

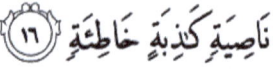

naa*s*iyatin~kaadzibatin khoo*t*i a*h*

A lying, sinning forelock

Chapter 96: Surat Al-`Alaq (The Clot)- 19 aayats in total

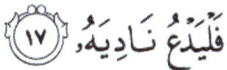

fal yad'u naadiya*h*
Then let him call his associates;

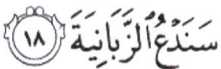

sanad'uz zabaaniya*h*
We will call the angels of Hell

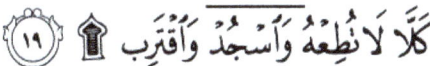

kallaa laa tu*t*i'*h*u wasjud waqtarib
No! Do not obey him. But prostrate and draw near [to Allah]

Worship Allah and associate nothing with Him, and to parents do good, and to relatives, orphans, the needy, the near neighbor, the neighbor farther away, the companion at your side, the traveler, and those whom your right hands possess. Indeed, Allah does not like those who are self-deluding and boastful (4:36 An-Nisa`)

Chapter 97: Surat Al-Qadr (The Power) - 5 aayats in total

بسم الله الرحمن الرحيم

إِنَّآ أَنزَلْنَٰهُ فِى لَيْلَةِ ٱلْقَدْرِ ﴿١﴾

innaaa an~zalnaa*hu* fii lailatil qadr
Indeed, We sent the Qur'an down during the Night of Decree

وَمَآ أَدْرَىٰكَ مَا لَيْلَةُ ٱلْقَدْرِ ﴿٢﴾

wa maaa adrooka maa lailatul qadr
And what can make you know what is the Night of Decree

لَيْلَةُ ٱلْقَدْرِ خَيْرٌ مِّنْ أَلْفِ شَهْرٍ ﴿٣﴾

lailatul qadri khoirum min alfi sha*hr*
The Night of Decree is better than a thousand months

نَنزَّلُ ٱلْمَلَٰٓئِكَةُ وَٱلرُّوحُ فِيهَا بِإِذْنِ رَبِّهِم مِّن كُلِّ أَمْرٍ ﴿٤﴾

tanazzalul malaaa ikatu war ruuhu fii*h*aa bi idzni robbi*h*im min~kulli amr
The angels and the Spirit descend therein by permission of their Lord for every matter

سَلَٰمٌ هِىَ حَتَّىٰ مَطْلَعِ ٱلْفَجْرِ ﴿٥﴾

salaamun *h*iya hattaa ma*t*la'il fajr
Peace it is until the emergence of dawn

Chapter 98: Surat Al-Bayyinah (The Clear Proof) - 8 aayats in total

بسم الله الرحمن الرحيم

لَمْ يَكُنِ ٱلَّذِينَ كَفَرُوا۟ مِنْ أَهْلِ ٱلْكِتَـٰبِ وَٱلْمُشْرِكِينَ مُنفَكِّينَ حَتَّىٰ تَأْتِيَهُمُ ٱلْبَيِّنَةُ ۝

lam yakunil ladziina kafaruu min a*h*lil kitaabi wal mushrikiina mun~fakkiina hattaa ta*k*tiya*h*umul bayyina*h*

Those who disbelieved among the People of the Scripture and the polytheists were not to be parted [from misbelief] until there came to them clear evidence

رَسُولٌ مِّنَ ٱللَّهِ يَتْلُوا۟ صُحُفًا مُّطَهَّرَةً ۝

rosuulum min*allaah*i yatluu *s*uhufam mu*t*o*hh*aro*h*

A Messenger from Allah, reciting purified scriptures

فِيهَا كُتُبٌ قَيِّمَةٌ ۝

fii*h*aa kutubun~qoyyima*h*

Within which are correct writings

وَمَا تَفَرَّقَ ٱلَّذِينَ أُوتُوا۟ ٱلْكِتَـٰبَ إِلَّا مِنۢ بَعْدِ مَا جَآءَتْهُمُ ٱلْبَيِّنَةُ ۝

wa maa tafarroqol ladziina uutul kitaaba illaa mim ba'di maa jaaa at *h*umul bayyina*h*

Nor did those who were given the Scripture become divided until after there had come to them clear evidence

Chapter 98: Surat Al-Bayyinah (The Clear Proof) - 8 aayats in total

وَمَآ أُمِرُوٓاْ إِلَّا لِيَعْبُدُواْ ٱللَّهَ مُخْلِصِينَ لَهُ ٱلدِّينَ حُنَفَآءَ وَيُقِيمُواْ ٱلصَّلَوٰةَ وَيُؤْتُواْ ٱلزَّكَوٰةَ وَذَٰلِكَ دِينُ ٱلْقَيِّمَةِ ٥

wa maaa umiruuu illaa liya'bud*ullaah*a muk*h*li*s*iina la*h*ud diina hunafaaa a wa yuqiimu*s* *s*olaata wa yu*k*tuz zakaata wa dzaalika diinul qoyyima*h*

And they were not commanded except to worship Allah, [being] sincere to Him in religion, inclining to truth, and to establish prayer and to give zakah. And that is the correct religion

إِنَّ ٱلَّذِينَ كَفَرُواْ مِنْ أَهْلِ ٱلْكِتَٰبِ وَٱلْمُشْرِكِينَ فِى نَارِ جَهَنَّمَ خَٰلِدِينَ فِيهَآ أُوْلَٰٓئِكَ هُمْ شَرُّ ٱلْبَرِيَّةِ ٦

innal ladziina kafaruu min a*h*lil kitaabi wal mushrikiina fii naari ja*h*annama khoolidiina fii*h*aaa ulaaa ika *h*um sharrul bariyya*h*

Indeed, they who disbelieved among the People of the Scripture and the polytheists will be in the fire of Hell, abiding eternally therein. Those are the worst of creatures.

Chapter 98: Surat Al-Bayyinah (The Clear Proof) - 8 aayats in total

إِنَّ ٱلَّذِينَ ءَامَنُوا۟ وَعَمِلُوا۟ ٱلصَّٰلِحَٰتِ أُو۟لَٰٓئِكَ هُمْ خَيْرُ ٱلْبَرِيَّةِ ۝

innal ladziina aamanuu wa 'amilus soolihaati ulaaa ika hum khoirul bariyyah

Indeed, they who have believed and done righteous deeds - those are the best of creatures

جَزَآؤُهُمْ عِندَ رَبِّهِمْ جَنَّٰتُ عَدْنٍ تَجْرِى مِن تَحْتِهَا ٱلْأَنْهَٰرُ خَٰلِدِينَ فِيهَآ أَبَدًا رَّضِىَ ٱللَّهُ عَنْهُمْ وَرَضُوا۟ عَنْهُ ذَٰلِكَ لِمَنْ خَشِىَ رَبَّهُۥ ۝

jazaaa u hum 'inda robbihim jannaatu 'adnin~tajrii min~tahtihal anhaaru khoolidiina fiihaaa abada. rodiyallaahu 'anhum wa roduu 'anhu dzaalika liman khoshiya robbah

Their reward with Allah will be gardens of perpetual residence beneath which rivers flow, wherein they will abide forever, Allah being pleased with them and they with Him. That is for whoever has feared his Lord

And of His signs is that He created for you from yourselves mates that you may find tranquillity in them; and He placed between you affection and mercy. Indeed in that are signs for a people who give thought
(30:21 Ar-Rum)

Chapter 99: Surat Az-Zalzalah (The Earthquake) - 8 aayats in total

بسم الله الرحمن الرحيم

إِذَا زُلْزِلَتِ ٱلْأَرْضُ زِلْزَالَهَا ١

idzaa zulzilatil ar*du* zilzaala*h*aa

When the earth is shaken with its [final] earthquake

وَأَخْرَجَتِ ٱلْأَرْضُ أَثْقَالَهَا ٢

wa akhrojatil ar*du* athqoola*h*aa

And the earth discharges its burdens

وَقَالَ ٱلْإِنسَٰنُ مَا لَهَا ٣

wa qoolal in~saanu maa la*h*aa

And man says, what is [wrong] with it

يَوْمَئِذٍ تُحَدِّثُ أَخْبَارَهَا ٤

yauma idzin~tuhaddithu akhbaaro*h*aa

That Day, it will report its news

بِأَنَّ رَبَّكَ أَوْحَىٰ لَهَا ٥

bi anna robbaka auhaa la*h*aa

Because your Lord has commanded it

Chapter 99: Surat Az-Zalzalah (The Earthquake) - 8 aayats in total

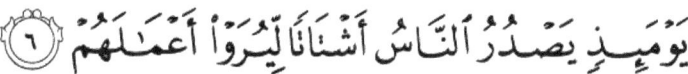

yauma idziy ya_s_durun naasu ashtaatal liyurau a'maala_h_um

That Day, the people will depart separated [into categories] to be shown [the result of] their deeds

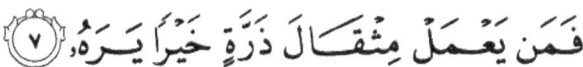

fa may ya'mal mithqoola dzarrotin khoiroy yaro_h_

So whoever does an atom's weight of good will see it

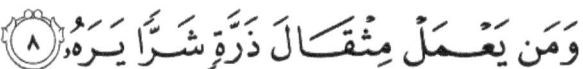

wa may ya'mal mithqoola dzarrotin~sharroy yaro_h_

And whoever does an atom's weight of evil will see it

Exalted is He who created all pairs - from what the earth grows and from themselves and from that which they do not know (36:36 Ya-Sin)

Chapter 100: Surat Al-ʿĀdiyāt (The Courser) - 11 aayats in total

بسم الله الرحمن الرحيم

وَٱلۡعَٰدِيَٰتِ ضَبۡحًا ١

wal 'aadiyaati _d_ob haa

By the racers, panting

فَٱلۡمُورِيَٰتِ قَدۡحًا ٢

fal muuriyaati qod haa

And the producers of sparks [when] striking

فَٱلۡمُغِيرَٰتِ صُبۡحًا ٣

fal mughiirooti _s_ub haa

And the chargers at dawn

فَأَثَرۡنَ بِهِۦ نَقۡعًا ٤

fa atharna bi_h_ii naq'aa

Stirring up thereby [clouds of] dust

فَوَسَطۡنَ بِهِۦ جَمۡعًا ٥

fa wasa_t_na bi_h_ii jam'aa

Arriving thereby in the center collectively

إِنَّ ٱلۡإِنسَٰنَ لِرَبِّهِۦ لَكَنُودٌ ٦

innal in~saana lirobbi_h_ii lakanuud

Indeed mankind, to his Lord, is ungrateful

Chapter 100: Surat Al-ʿĀdiyāt (The Courser) - 11 aayats in total

wa inna*h*uu 'alaa dzaalika lasha*h*iid

And indeed, he is to that a witness

wa inna*h*uu lihubbil khoiri lashadiid

And indeed he is, in love of wealth, intense

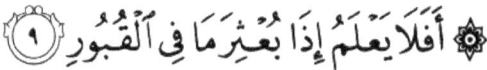

afalaa ya'lamu idzaa bu'thiro maa fil qubuur

But does he not know that when the contents of the graves are scattered

wa hu*ss*ila maa fi*s* *s*uduur

And that within the breasts is obtained

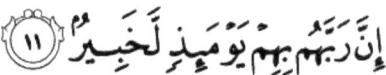

inna robba*h*um bi*h*im yauma idzil lakhobiir

Indeed, their Lord with them, that Day, is [fully] Acquainted

بسم الله الرحمن الرحيم

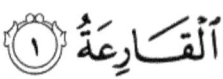

al qoori'a<u>h</u>

The Striking Calamity

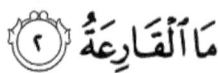

mal qoori'a<u>h</u>

What is the Striking Calamity

وَمَآ أَدْرَىٰكَ مَا ٱلْقَارِعَةُ ۝

wa maaa adrooka mal qoori'a<u>h</u>

And what can make you know what is the Striking Calamity

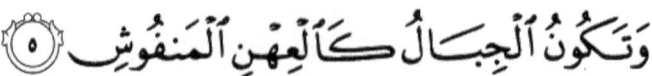

yauma yakuunun naasu kal farooshil mabthuuth

It is the Day when people will be like moths, dispersed

وَتَكُونُ ٱلْجِبَالُ كَٱلْعِهْنِ ٱلْمَنفُوشِ ۝

wa takuunul jibaalu kal 'i<u>h</u>nil man~fuush

And the mountains will be like wool, fluffed up

Chapter 101: Surat Al-Qāri`ah (The Calamity) - 11 aayats in total

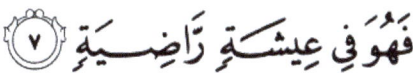

fa ammaa man~thaqulat mawaaziinu*h*

Then as for one whose scales are heavy [with good deeds]

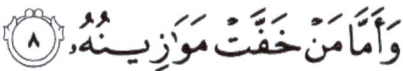

fa *h*uwa fii 'iishatir roo*d*iya*h*

He will be in a pleasant life

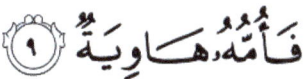

wa ammaa man khoffat mawaaziinu*h*

But as for one whose scales are light

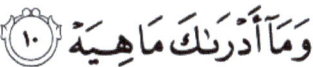

fa ummu*h*uu *h*aawiya*h*

His refuge will be an abyss

wa maaa adrooka maa *h*iya*h*

And what can make you know what that is

naarun haamiya*h*

It is a Fire, intensely hot

Chapter 102: Surat At-Takāthur (The Rivalry world increase) - 8 aayats in total

بسم الله الرحمن الرحيم

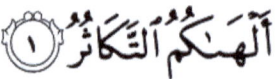

al *h*aakumut takaathur

Competition in [worldly] increase diverts you

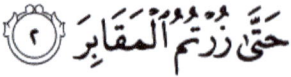

hattaa zurtumul maqoobir

Until you visit the graveyards

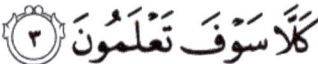

kallaa saufa ta'lamuun

No! You are going to know

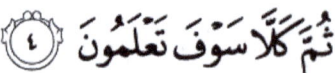

thumma kallaa saufa ta'lamuun

Then no! You are going to know

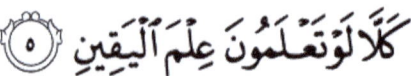

kallaa lau ta'lamuuna 'ilmal yaqiin

No! If you only knew with knowledge of certainty

Chapter 102: Surat At-Takāthur (The Rivalry world increase) - 8 aayats in total

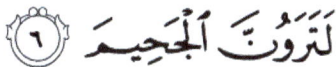

latarawunnal jahiim

You will surely see the Hellfire

thumma latarawunna*h*aa 'ainal yaqiin

Then you will surely see it with the eye of certainty

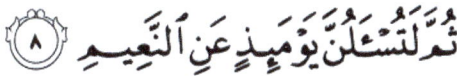

thumma latus alunna yauma idzin 'anin na'iim

Then you will surely be asked that Day about pleasure

If you disclose your charitable expenditures, they are good; but if you conceal them and give them to the poor, it is better for you, and He will remove from you some of your misdeeds [thereby]. And Allah, with what you do, is [fully] Acquainted (2:271 Al-Baqarah)

Chapter 103: Surat Al-`Aṣr (The Declining Day) - 3 aayats in total

بسم الله الرحمن الرحيم

وَٱلْعَصْرِ ﴿١﴾

wal 'aṣr

By time

إِنَّ ٱلْإِنسَٰنَ لَفِى خُسْرٍ ﴿٢﴾

innal in~saana lafii khusr

Indeed, mankind is in loss

إِلَّا ٱلَّذِينَ ءَامَنُوا۟ وَعَمِلُوا۟ ٱلصَّٰلِحَٰتِ وَتَوَاصَوْا۟ بِٱلْحَقِّ وَتَوَاصَوْا۟ بِٱلصَّبْرِ ﴿٣﴾

illal ladziina aamanuu wa 'amilus ṣoolihaati wa tawaaṣau bil haqqi wa tawaaṣau bis ṣobr

Except for those who have believed and done righteous deeds and advised each other to truth and advised each other to patience

And We have certainly made the Qur'an easy for remembrance, so is there any who will remember? (54:32 Al-Qamar)

Chapter 104: Surat Al-Humazah (The Traducer) - 9 aayats in total

بسم الله الرحمن الرحيم

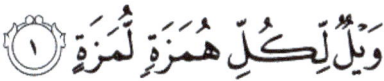

wailul likulli _h_umazatil lumaza_h_

Woe to every scorner and mocker

وَعَدَّدَهُ مَالَا جَمَعَ الَّذِى

al ladzii jama'a maalau wa 'addada_h_

Who collects wealth and [continuously] counts it

أَخْلَدَهُ مَالَهُ أَنَّ يَحْسَبُ

yahsabu anna maala_h_uuu akhlada_h_

He thinks that his wealth will make him immortal

الْحُطَمَةِ فِى لَيُنْبَذَنَّ كَلَّا

kallaa layumbadzanna fil hu_t_oma_h_

No! He will surely be thrown into the Crusher

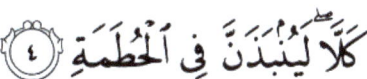

wa maaa adrooka mal hu_t_oma_h_

And what can make you know what is the Crusher

Chapter 104: Surat Al-Humazah (The Traducer) - 9 aayats in total

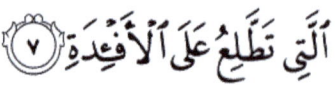

naar*ullaah*il muuqoda*h*

It is the fire of Allah, [eternally] fueled

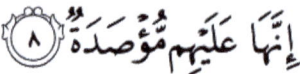

al latii ta*tt*oli'u 'alal af ida*h*

Which mounts directed at the hearts

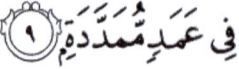

inna*h*aa 'alai*h*im mu*k*soda*h*

Indeed, Hellfire will be closed down upon them

fii 'amadim mumaddada*h*

In extended columns

It is He who made the sun a shining light and the moon a derived light and determined for it phases - that you may know the number of years and account [of time]. Allah has not created this except in truth. He details the signs for a people who know (10:5 Yunus)

Chapter 105: Surat Al-Fīl (The Elephant) - 5 aayats in total

بسم الله الرحمن الرحيم

أَلَمْ تَرَ كَيْفَ فَعَلَ رَبُّكَ بِأَصْحَابِ ٱلْفِيلِ ﴿١﴾

alam tarokaifa fa'ala robbuka bi a<u>s</u> haabil fiil

Have you not considered, [O Muhammad], how your Lord dealt with the companions of the elephant

أَلَمْ يَجْعَلْ كَيْدَهُمْ فِي تَضْلِيلٍ ﴿٢﴾

alam yaj'al kaida <u>h</u>um fi ta<u>d</u>liil

Did He not make their plan into misguidance

وَأَرْسَلَ عَلَيْهِمْ طَيْرًا أَبَابِيلَ ﴿٣﴾

wa arsala 'alai<u>h</u>im <u>t</u>oiron abaabiil

And He sent against them birds in flocks

تَرْمِيهِم بِحِجَارَةٍ مِّن سِجِّيلٍ ﴿٤﴾

tarmii<u>h</u>im bi hijaarotim min~sijjiil

Striking them with stones of hard clay

فَجَعَلَهُمْ كَعَصْفٍ مَّأْكُولٍ ﴿٥﴾

fa ja'ala<u>h</u>um ka'a<u>s</u>fim ma<u>kk</u>uul

And He made them like eaten straw

Chapter 106: Surat Quraysh (Quraysh) - 4 aayats in total

بسم الله الرحمن الرحيم

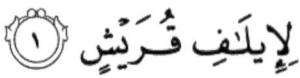

li iilaafi quroish

For the accustomed security of the Quraysh

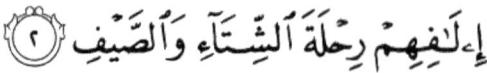

iilaafi*h*im rihlatash shitaaa i wa*s* *s*oiif

Their accustomed security [in] the caravan of winter and summer

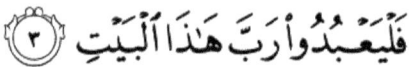

fal ya'buduu robba *h*aadzal baiit

Let them worship the Lord of this House

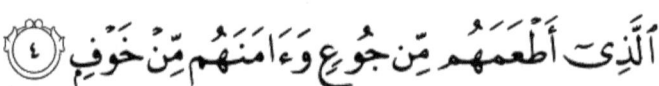

al ladziii a*t*'ama*h*um min~juu'iw wa aamana*h*um min khouuf

Who has fed them, [saving them] from hunger and made them safe, [saving them] from fear

How can you disbelieve in Allah when you were lifeless and He brought you to life; then He will cause you to die, then He will bring you [back] to life, and then to Him you will be returned (2:28 Al-Baqarah)

Chapter 107: Surat Al-Mā`ūn (The Small Kindnesses) - 7 aayats in total

بسم الله الرحمن الرحيم

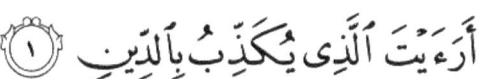

aro aital ladzii yukadzzibu bid diin
Have you seen the one who denies the Recompense

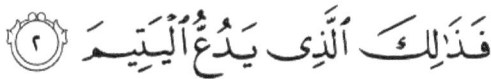

fa dzaalikal ladzii yadu' 'ul yatiim
For that is the one who drives away the orphan

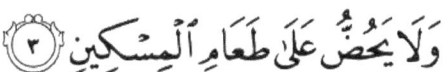

wa laa yahuddu 'alaa to'aamil miskiin
And does not encourage the feeding of the poor

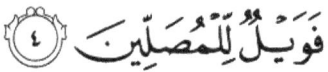

fa wailul lilmusolliin
So woe to those who pray

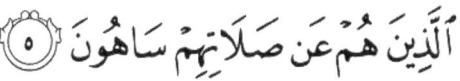

al ladziina hum 'an~solaatihim saahuun
[But] who are heedless of their prayer

Chapter 107: Surat Al-Mā`ūn (The Small Kindnesses) - 7 aayats in total

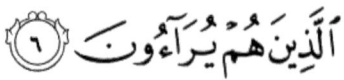

al ladziina *h*um yurooo uun

Those who make show [of their deeds]

wa yamna'uunal maa'uun

And withhold [simple] assistance

And if Allah were to impose blame on the people for their wrongdoing, He would not have left upon the earth any creature, but He defers them for a specified term. And when their term has come, they will not remain behind an hour, nor will they precede [it] (16:61 An-Nahl)

Chapter 108: Surat Al-Kawthar (The Abundance) - 3 aayats in total

بسم الله الرحمن الرحيم

innaaa a'_t_oynaakal kauthar

Indeed, We have granted you, [O Muhammad], al-Kawthar

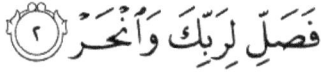

fa _s_olli lirobbika wan har

So pray to your Lord and sacrifice [to Him alone]

inna shaani aka _h_uwal abtar

Indeed, your enemy is the one cut off

To Allah belongs whatever is in the heavens and whatever is in the earth
Whether you show what is within yourselves or conceal it, Allah will bring
you to account for it Then He will forgive whom He wills and punish
whom He wills, and Allah is over all things competent
(2:284 Al-Baqarah)

Chapter 109: Surat Al-Kāfirūn (The Disbelievers) - 6 aayats in total

بسم الله الرحمن الرحيم

قُلْ يَٰٓأَيُّهَا ٱلْكَٰفِرُونَ ﴿١﴾

qul yaaa ayyuhal kaafiruun

Say, O disbelievers

لَآ أَعْبُدُ مَا تَعْبُدُونَ ﴿٢﴾

laaa a'budu maa ta'buduun

I do not worship what you worship

وَلَآ أَنتُمْ عَٰبِدُونَ مَآ أَعْبُدُ ﴿٣﴾

walaaa an~tum 'aabiduuna maaa a'bud

Nor are you worshippers of what I worship

وَلَآ أَنَا۠ عَابِدٌ مَّا عَبَدتُّمْ ﴿٤﴾

wa laaa ana 'aabidum maa 'abadtum

Nor will I be a worshipper of what you worship

وَلَآ أَنتُمْ عَٰبِدُونَ مَآ أَعْبُدُ ﴿٥﴾

walaaa an~tum 'aabiduuna maaa a'bud

Nor will you be worshippers of what I worship

لَكُمْ دِينُكُمْ وَلِيَ دِينِ ﴿٦﴾

lakum diinukum wa liya diin

For you is your religion, and for me is my religion

Chapter 110: Surat An-Naṣr (The Divine Support) - 3 aayats in total

بسم الله الرحمن الرحيم

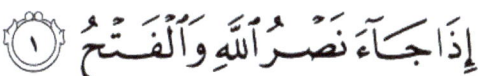

iza jaaa a na_s_r_ullaah_i wal fath

When the victory of Allah has come and the conquest

wa ro aitan naasa yadkhuluuna fii diin_illaah_i afwaaja

And you see the people entering into the religion of Allah in multitudes

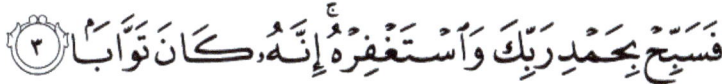

fa sabbih bihamdi robbika wastaghfir_hu_ inna_h_uu kaana tawwaaba

Then exalt [Him] with praise of your Lord and ask forgiveness of Him. Indeed, He is ever Accepting of repentance

Indeed, your Lord is Allah, who created the heavens and earth in six days and then established Himself above the Throne. He covers the night with the day, [another night] chasing it rapidly, and [He created] the sun, the moon, and the stars, subjected by His command. Unquestionably, His is the creation and the command; blessed is Allah, Lord of the worlds
(7:54 Aw-A'raf)

Chapter 111: Surat Al-Masad (The Palm Fiber, Flame) - 5 aayats in total

بسم الله الرحمن الرحيم

تَبَّتۡ یَدَاۤ أَبِی لَهَبٍ وَتَبَّ ۝١

tabbat yadaaa abii lahabiw wa tabb

May the hands of Abu Lahab be ruined, and ruined is he

مَاۤ أَغۡنَیٰ عَنۡهُ مَالُهُۥ وَمَا كَسَبَ ۝٢

maaa aghnaa 'anhu maaluhuu wa maa kasab

His wealth will not avail him or that which he gained

سَیَصۡلَیٰ نَارًا ذَاتَ لَهَبٍ ۝٣

sayaslaa naaron~dzaata lahab

He will [enter to] burn in a Fire of [blazing] flame

وَامۡرَأَتُهُۥ حَمَّالَةَ ٱلۡحَطَبِ ۝٤

wamro atuhuu hammaa latal hatob

And his wife [as well] - the carrier of firewood

فِی جِیدِهَا حَبۡلٌ مِّن مَّسَدٍ ۝٥

fii jiidihaa hablum mim masad

Around her neck is a rope of [twisted] fiber

Chapter 112: Surat Al-'Ikhlāṣ (The Sincerity) - 4 aayats in total

بسم الله الرحمن الرحيم

قُلْ هُوَ ٱللَّهُ أَحَدٌ ﴿١﴾

qul huwallaahu ahad

Say, He is Allah, [who is] One

ٱللَّهُ ٱلصَّمَدُ ﴿٢﴾

allaahus somad

Allah, the Eternal Refuge

لَمْ يَلِدْ وَلَمْ يُولَدْ ﴿٣﴾

lam yalid wa lam yuulad

He neither begets nor is born

وَلَمْ يَكُن لَّهُۥ كُفُوًا أَحَدٌۢ ﴿٤﴾

wa lam yakul lahuu kufuwan ahad

Nor is there to Him any equivalent

O you who have believed, seek help through patience and prayer. Indeed, Allah is with the patient (2:153 Al-Baqarah)

Chapter 113: Surat Al-Falaq (The Daybreak) - 5 aayats in total

بسم الله الرحمن الرحيم

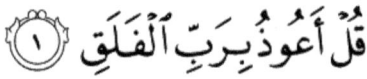

qul a'uudzu bi robbil falaq

Say, I seek refuge in the Lord of daybreak

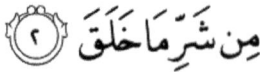

min~sharri maa kholaq

From the evil of that which He created

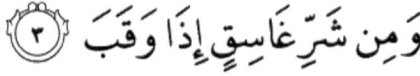

wa min~sharri ghoosikin idzaa waqab

And from the evil of darkness when it settles

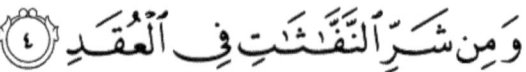

wa min~sharrin naffaathaati fil 'uqod

And from the evil of the blowers in knots

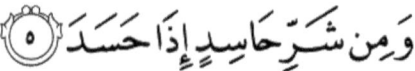

wa min~sharri haasidin idzaa hasad

And from the evil of an envier when he envies

Chapter 114: Surat An-Nās (The Mankind)- 6 aayats in total

بسم الله الرحمن الرحيم

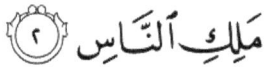

qul a'uudzu birobbin naas

Say, I seek refuge in the Lord of mankind

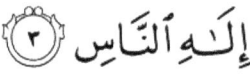

malikin naas

The Sovereign of mankind

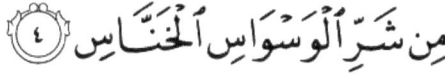

ilaahin naas

The God of mankind

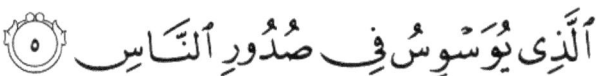

min~sharril waswaasil khonnaas

From the evil of the retreating whisperer

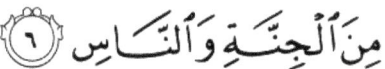

al ladzii yuwaswisu fii suduurin naas

Who whispers [evil] into the breasts of mankind

minal jinnati wannaas

From among the jinn and mankind

arabic letters

Final	Medial	Initial
ل	░░░	ا
ب	ب	ب
ت	ت	ت
ث	ث	ث
ج	ج	ج
ح	ح	ح
خ	خ	خ
د	░░░	د
ذ	░░░	ذ

Isolated	Name
ا	alif
ب	ba
ت	ta
ث	tha
ج	jim
ح	ha
خ	kho
د	dal
ذ	dzal

arabic letters

Final	Medial	Initial
ﺮ		ﺭ
ﺰ		ﺯ
ﺲ	ﺴ	ﺳ
ﺶ	ﺸ	ﺷ
ﺺ	ﺼ	ﺻ
ﺾ	ﻀ	ﺿ
ﻂ	ﻄ	ﻃ
ﻆ	ﻈ	ﻇ
ﻊ	ﻌ	ﻋ

Isolated	Name
ﺭ	ro
ﺯ	zai
ﺱ	sin
ﺵ	shin
ﺹ	sod
ﺽ	dod
ﻁ	to
ﻅ	zo
ﻉ	'ain

a r a b i c   l e t t e r s

Final	Medial	Initial
ـغ	ـغـ	غـ
ـف	ـفـ	فـ
ـق	ـقـ	قـ
ـك	ـكـ	كـ
ـل	ـلـ	لـ
ـم	ـمـ	مـ
ـن	ـنـ	نـ
ـه	ـهـ	هـ
ـو		و

Isolated	Name
غ	ghain
ف	fa
ق	qof
ك	kaf
ل	lam
م	mim
ن	nun
ه	ha
و	waw

a r a b i c   l e t t e r s

Final	Medial	Initial
لا	▨	لا
ـي	ـيـ	يـ
placed above or below other alphabet		

Isolated	Name
لا	lam alif
ي	ya
ء	hamza

N O T E S

···

···

···

···

···

···

···

···

45

phonetic guide

a / aa / aaa
pronounce as if the word "are". Same letters back to back indicating a longer sound count.

i / ii / iii
pronounce as if the word "bee" without the letter "b". Same letters back to back indicating a longer sound count.

o / oo / ooo
pronounce as if the word "awe". Same letters back to back indicating a longer sound count.

u / uu / uuu
pronounce as if the word "zoo" without the letter "z". Same letters back to back indicating a longer sound count.

_d_ = arabic letter (ض)
pronounce as if the letter "d" but with thicker and heavier sound.

_h_ = arabic letter (ه)
pronounce as if the letter "h" but with thicker and heavier sound.

_k_ = arabic letter (ع)
pronounce as if the letter "k" but with hanging end sound.

_s_ = arabic letter (ص)
pronounce as if the letter "s" but with thicker and heavier sound.

_t_ = arabic letter (ط)
pronounce as if the letter "t" but with thicker and heavier sound.

_z_ = arabic letter (ظ)
pronounce as if the letter "z" but with thicker and heavier sound.

illaah / allaah / ullaah

special symbol for Allah's name which require the reader to listen to audio to fully appreciate this sound.

(~) symbol

This require "ghunnah" or nasalisation hold for 2 counts.

(') symbol

This represent the arabic letter 'ain (ع) where specific sound is produced.

N O T E S

....

....

....

....

....

....

....

....

....

....

....